Snails in shells

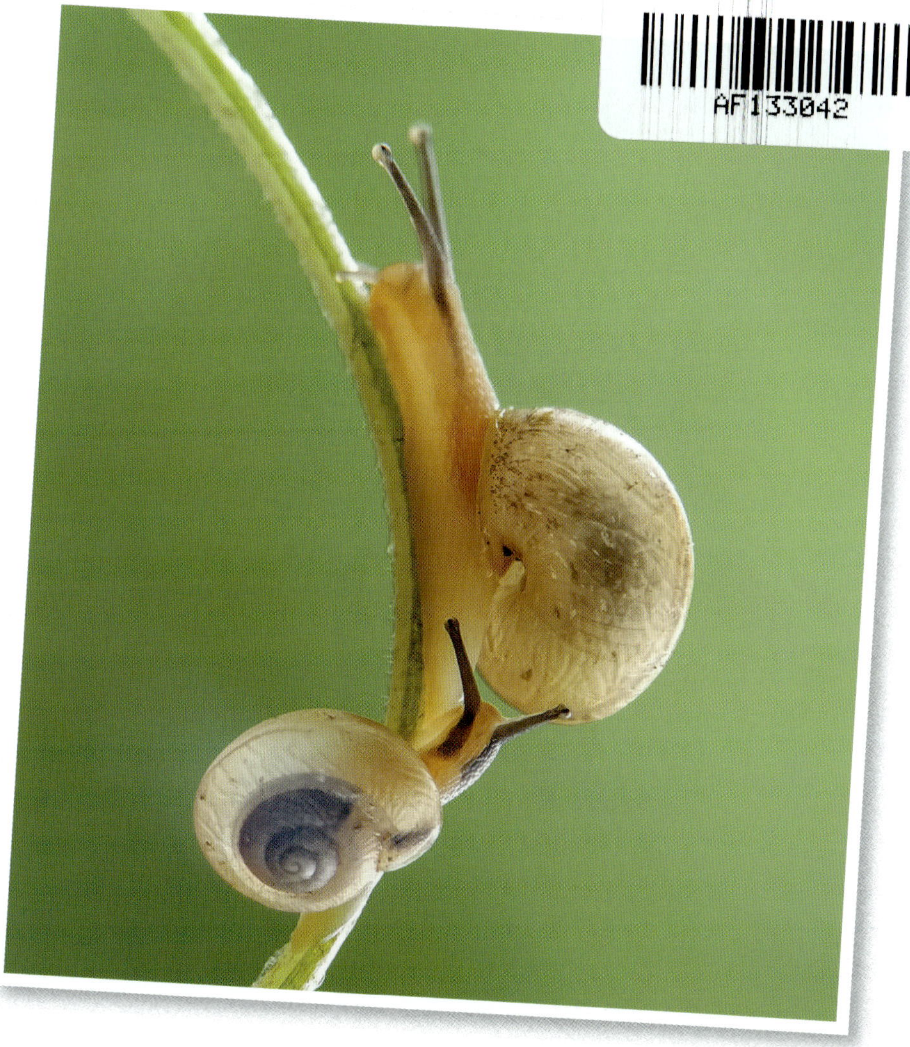

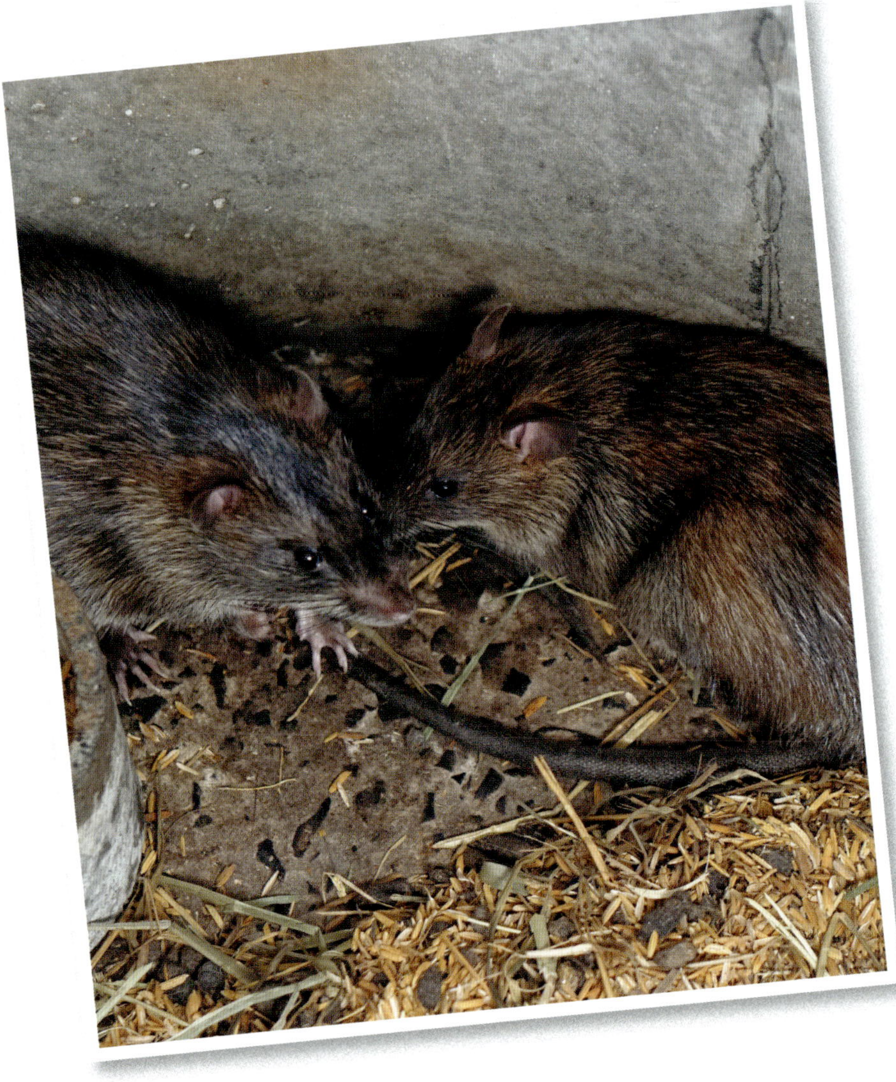

Rats in a den

Foxes in a den, too!

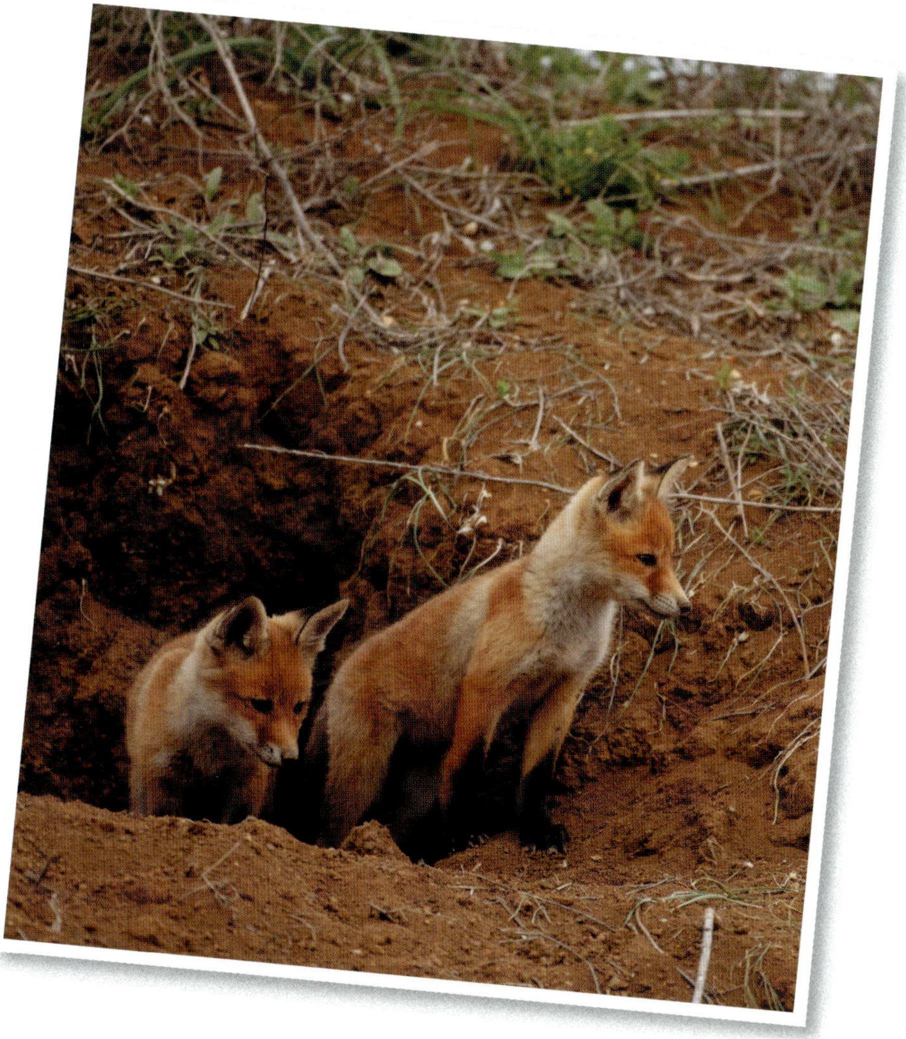

Otters in a holt

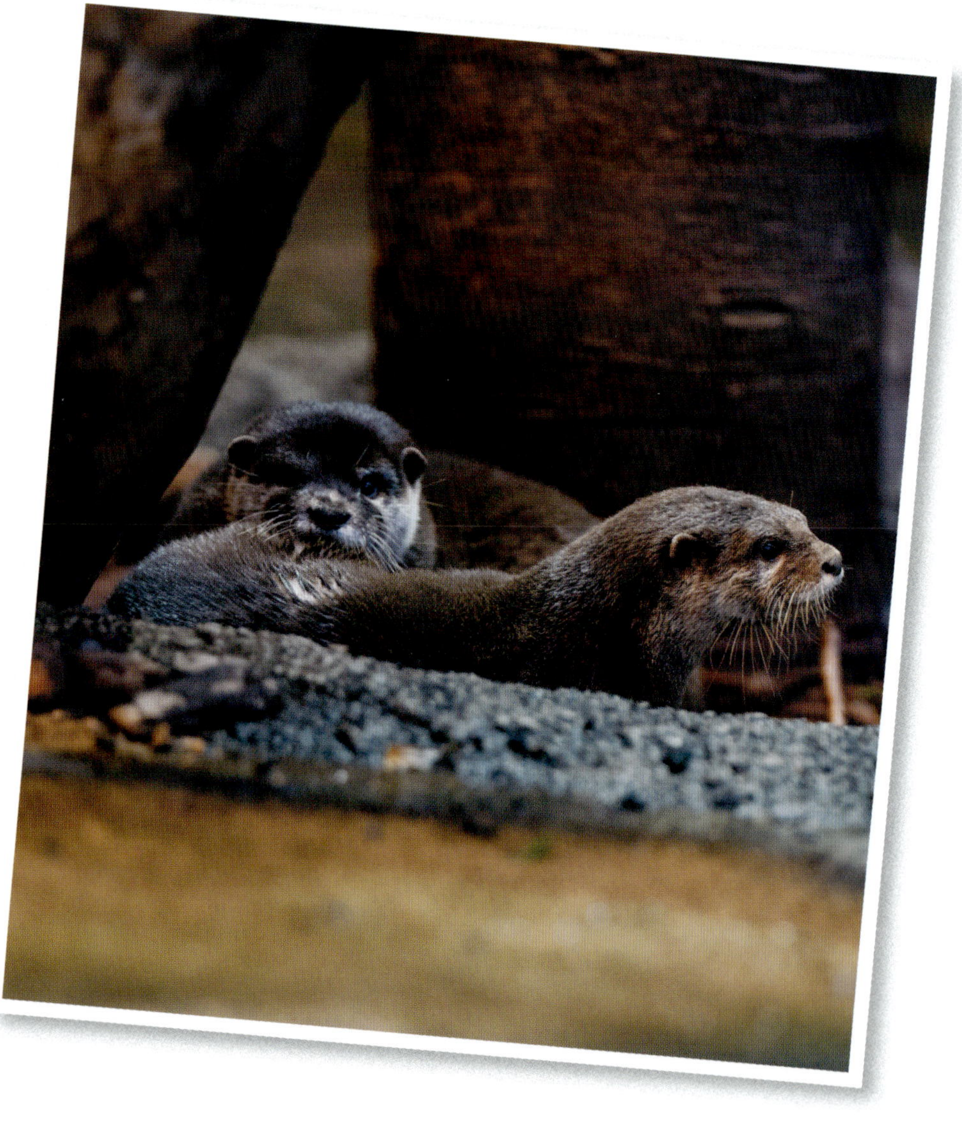

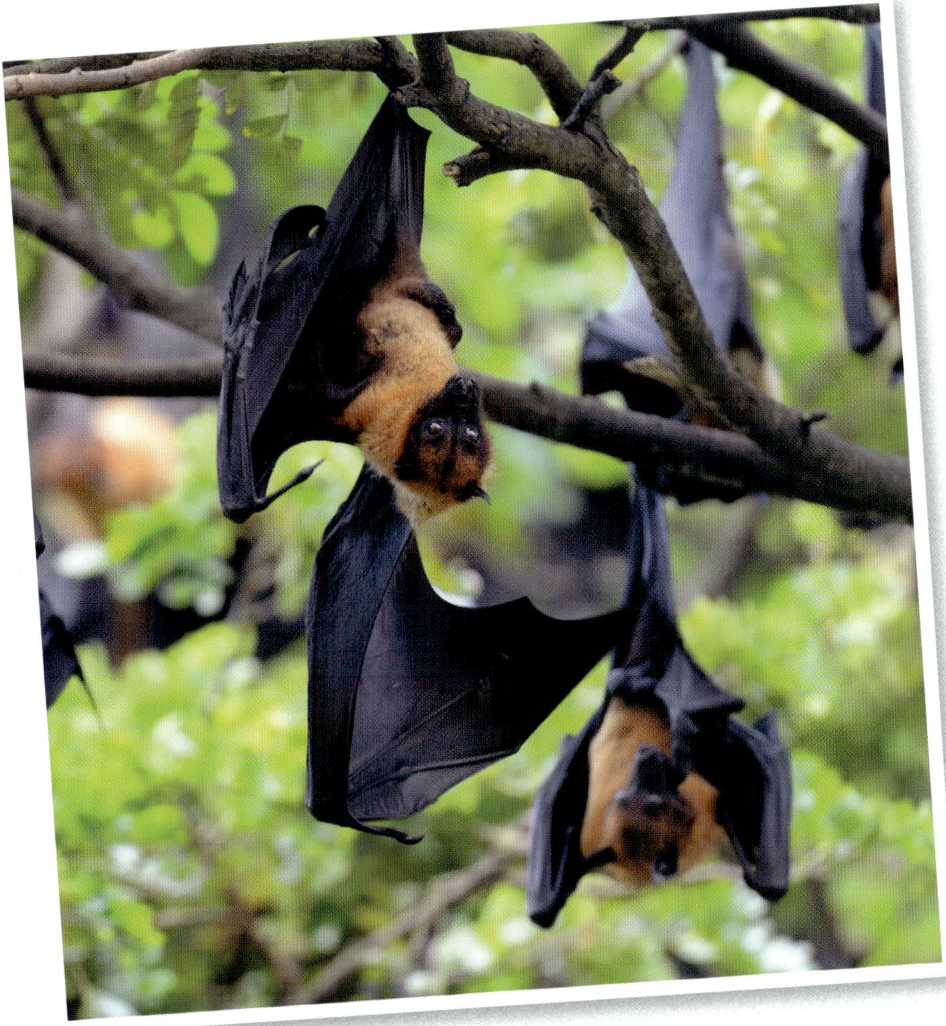

Bats roost in trees.

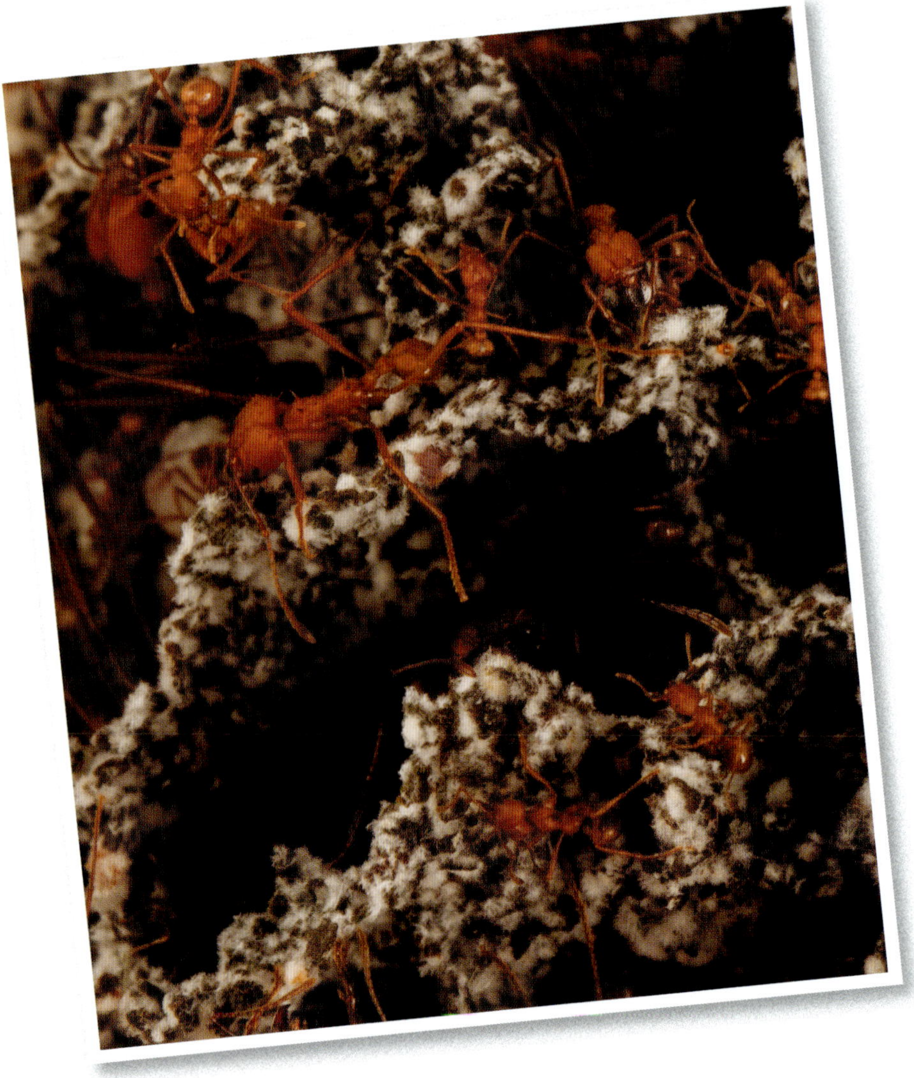

Ants in a nest

A duck on her nest

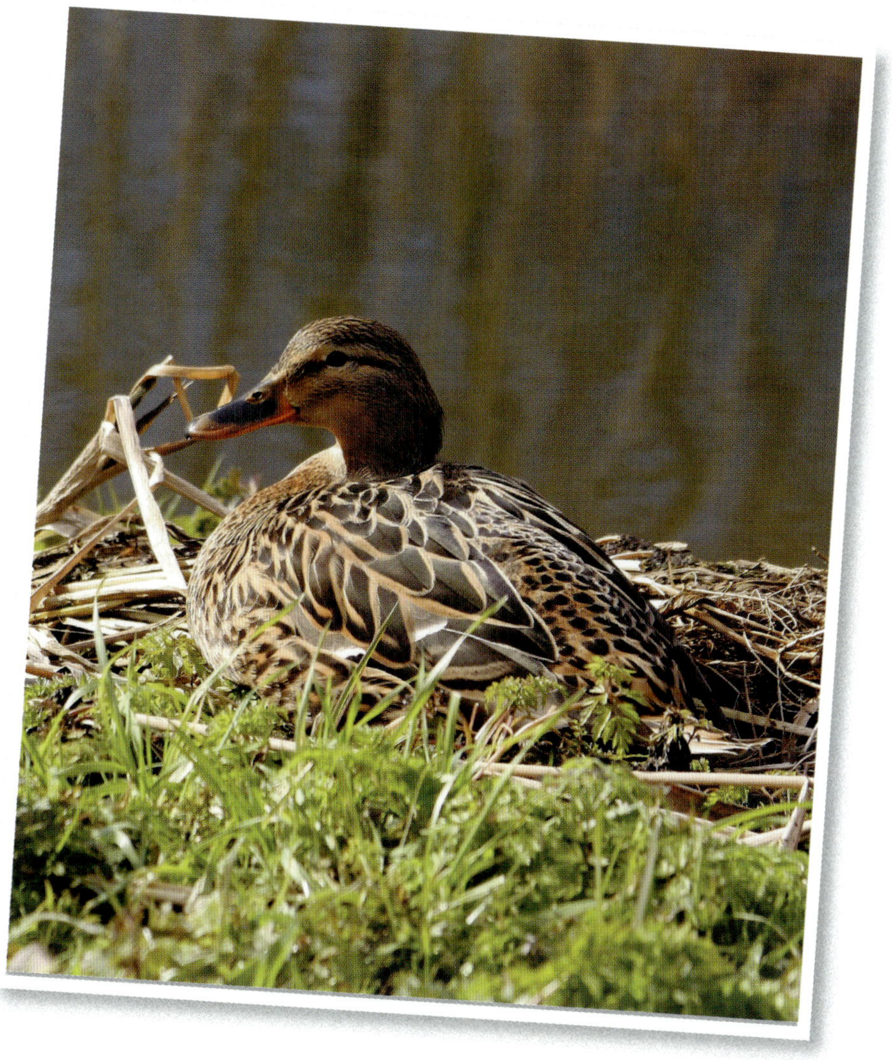

A gorilla in her nest, too!

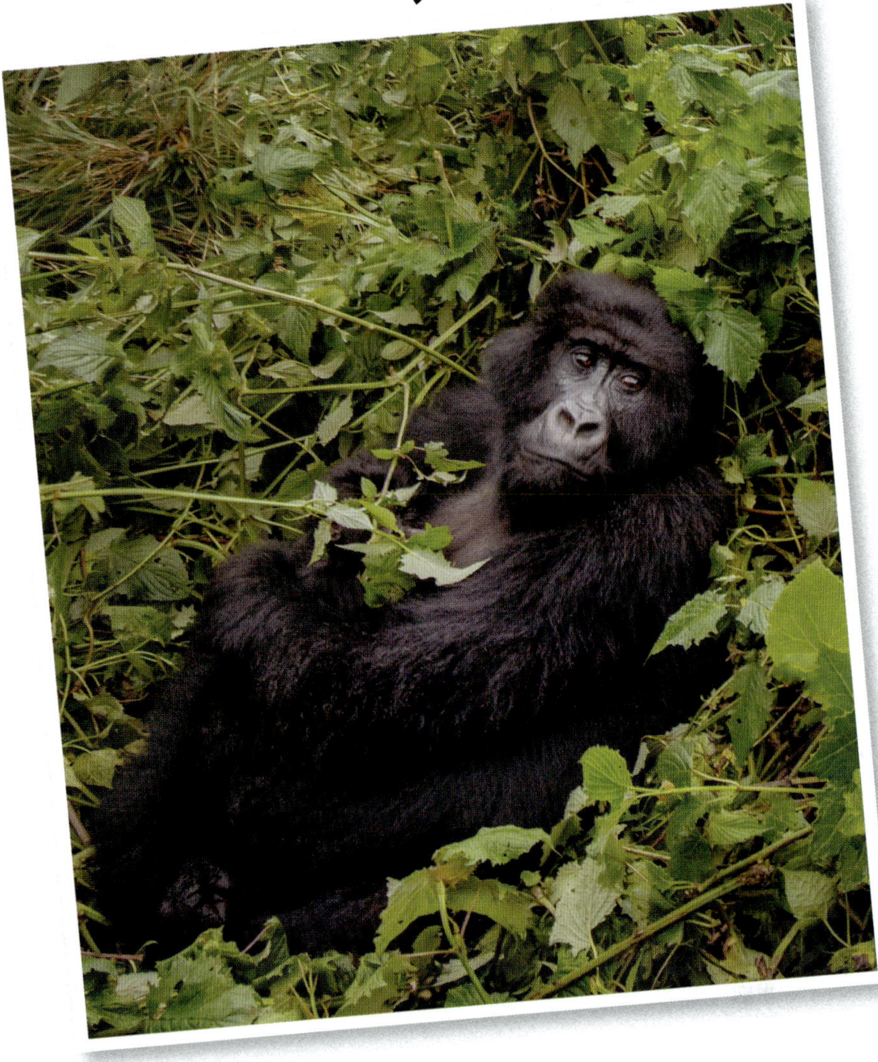